HEADLINES IV:
THE NEXT GENERATION

MORE OUT-OF-THIS-WORLD HEADLINES FROM THE BESTSELLING SERIES

COMPILED BY JAY LENO

WITH PHOTOGRAPHS BY JOSEPH DEL VALLE AND CARTOONS BY JACK DAVIS

WARNER BOOKS

A Time Warner Company

All author royalties will be donated to the Samuel Jared Kushnick Foundation, which funds pediatric A.I.D.S. programs and pediatric immunology research.

Warner Books, Inc., 1271 Avenue of the Americas, New York, NY 10020

Ⓦ A Time Warner Company

Printed in the United States of America
First Printing: December 1992
10 9 8 7 6 5 4 3 2 1

Library of Congress Cataloging in Publication Data

Headlines IV : the next generation : more out-of-this world headlines from the bestselling series / compiled by Jay Leno : with photographs by Joseph Del Valle and cartoons by Jack Davis.
    p.   cm.
  ISBN 0-446-39417-3
  1. Newspapers—Headlines—Humor. 2. American wit and humor. I. Leno, Jay. II. Title: Headlines four.
PN6231.N63H43   1992
081—dc20   92-16051
                                      CIP

Cover design by Jackie Merri Meyer and Robert Cuevas

Cover photography by Jay P. Morgan

Book design by Giorgetta Bell McRee

The publication of this latest HEADLINES book gives me the opportunity to thank the Tonight Show prop department for keeping all the headlines organized so that they can make it from show to book.

So thanks to Greg Elliott, Greg Dibene and Joe Drago.

—Jay Leno

1

You see them every time you pick up the paper—headlines that make you wonder whether you've inadvertently bought one of those supermarket tabloids. But it's *not* a tabloid, and these headlines *are* real. It's enough to make anyone ask:

WHAT'S THE WORLD COMING TO?

Daily BLAH

JAPANESE BUY WHITE HOUSE

From the "Did you look under your hat?" department:

Wife sues over lost brain

Honesty tests for workers can't be trusted, report says

If you can't trust an honesty test, what can you trust?

Dallas Woman Sucks Up 16 Lb. Bowling Ball

Think this woman has trouble getting dates?

It's Illegal to Sleep With Alligators

Miami

An appeals court has ruled illegal what many people assumed — you should not keep alligators in bed.

The ruling followed an appeal by , whose two alligators had been taken from him by officers who found him bleeding in bed from gator bites.

Talk about unsafe sex...

Arsonist elected fire department chief

CHESNEE (AP) —A 22-year-old convicted arsonist who is still on probation was unanimously elected chief of the Chesnee Volunteer Fire Department.

Michael Haynes has more than six years' experience putting out fires for the department. He also has experience setting them.

He was tried and convicted on six arson charges in Spartanburg and Cherokee counties in 1987, court records show.

Hey, Chief. I've got a date next Wednesday. Can we move the warehouse fire to Friday?

LCISD dress code insists on clean-shaven kindergarteners

I've heard of getting left back one grade, but this is ridiculous.

Dogs barred from Dog Museum

ST. LOUIS — Dogs are no longer welcome on the carpet at the Dog Museum.

The reason: too many canine accidents and too many fleas.

It used to be that dogs on leashes could browse through galleries full of paintings, sculptures and photographs of dogs.

But then, "You'd walk into a gallery and you'd see a big wet spot there, and you'd say, 'Oh, great,'" said Gail Haynes, the museum's business manager.

Not only that, but fleas left behind by shaggy visitors were biting the ankles of museum workers.

First preschoolers have to shave. Now dogs are being barred from their own museum. Our First Amendment rights are being trampled on!

Man who killed roommate is looking for place to live

Staff Writer

A Bardstown man who pleaded guilty but mentally ill to a charge of second—degree manslaughter is still looking for living arrangements so he can be released on probation.

Just don't argue with him over the remote control for the TV and everything will be fine.

'Dream date' woman gets money back from charity

By Jennifer Gould, Toronto Star

A woman who paid a Toronto charity $1,700 for a "dream date" received a full refund yesterday, after she learned the date didn't show because he was charged with attempted murder.

Brenda ██████, 38, attended the second annual Bachelor Auction of the Multiple Sclerosis Society's Toronto branch last fall.

Thousands of women were there to dole out money to the charity in exchange for being wined and dined by some of Metro's most eligible bachelors.

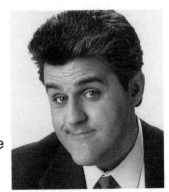

Gee, maybe she'd like a roommate instead.

Blaze destroys 97 vehicles at cookout held by firemen

Hey, has anybody seen the fire chief lately? (See page 6)

From the "Have a stroke, lose a stroke" department:

Man dies on golf course, but friends play through

WINTER HAVEN (AP) — Officials at a golf course covered Donald ~~DeGroote's~~ body with a sheet right where he died, on the 16th green. And the body stayed there two hours, while friends and neighbors played through.

"It was a real shock to all of us, but there really was nothing we could do," said golfer Robert ~~Alexander~~. "We all thought to ourselves, 'Gee, that's a good way to go.' He didn't suffer."

Kids must be shot by Monday

And clean shaven.

Brooksville buys shredder to aid record keeping

Hey, Bill. Where's the receipt for that shredder?

Former biology teacher finds he's happier running a brothel

PAHRUMP, Nev. — Russell ████ doesn't mind if you call him "madam," but he asks, "Make that Mr. Madam, if you will."

████ is indeed the madam, the person in charge at the Chicken Ranch, a brothel here in a desolate sagebrush valley northwest of Las Vegas.

It is a job he has had for eight years and to hear him tell it, it is a great line of work, much more rewarding than his former profession of high school biology teacher in his Sonoma County home town of Sebastopol.

Smoking allowed in the city sewers

CAMDENTON – The city will be testing some of its sewer lines Dec. 10 using a series of smoke bombs to detect leakage.

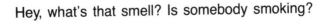

Hey, what's that smell? Is somebody smoking?

NEA discussing ban on spanking School officials,

Say, do you think that brothel-owning biology teacher is mixed up in this?

Unemployment not working, critics say

Maybe we're not giving it enough of a chance.

More than 33,000 vote for jail inmate

ST. PAUL (AP) — A jail inmate awaiting his second trial on a first-degree murder charge was the choice of 33,004 Minnesotans to serve as state treasurer.

He's tan, he's fit, he's ready. Nixon in '96.

Absentee Votes Accepted In Person Only

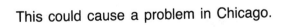

This could cause a problem in Chicago.

**"Great, just when I was about to water the lawn, it starts to rain"
department:**

Collapse may delay freeway demolition

Associated Press

SAN FRANCISCO — The collapse of a piece of the earthquake-damaged Embarcadero Freeway is likely to slow an already delayed demolition project, engineers say.

Man disputes government's claim he is dead

It's about time Strom Thurmond spoke out.

Study: People can delay death for important occasions

Chicago Tribune

CHICAGO — Death does take a holiday sometimes, sparing people until after they enjoy important festive occasions, researchers have concluded.

A study of death rates among elderly California Chinese women around the annual Harvest Moon Festival found that fewer women than normal died just before the holiday and deaths shot up briefly just after the festival's conclusion.

Yeah, like arguing with the government.

23

In District Court

Man told to get license so it can be suspended

But he can't get a license until he proves he's not dead, Your Honor.

Dr. Melinda Warner of Boston will be visiting her parents, **Mr. and Mrs. Daniel Warner** of Salem, N.H., for the holidays. She is a dropout from North Andover High.

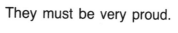

They must be very proud.

U.S. created 6.8 million secrets in '90

WASHINGTON — The U.S. government thinks it created about 6.8 million official secrets last year — although <u>it can't be sure because of government secrecy.</u>

Ssshhh!...

Secret math center to be located here

But you gotta promise not to tell anybody.

High-speed train could reach Valley within five years

PALMDALE — Within five years, Antelope Valley commuters could be spending less than $8 for a train ride to Los Angeles International Airport, a spokesman for the firm backing the high speed train said Thursday.

Five years? Well, it's still faster than Amtrak.

Quotables

"When they are dead, they're dead. We cannot do anything for your dead pets" — Homer Township Trustee Ethel Rodriguez, asking residents to stop bringing dead pets to the township recycling center.

The first rule of pet recycling: dogs with dogs, and cats with cats. No mixing.

It's a great after-school job.
Oh, sure, it doesn't pay much, but...

Naked woman stops at gasoline station

A woman in her mid-20s, nude except for a pair of shoes, walked into the Sinclair Service Station at 1703 14th St. N.W. about 12:30 a.m. Saturday and asked the cashier if it would be OK to clean her headlamps, Rochester police reported.

The cashier reported to the police that the nude woman then washed the headlights of her gray-colored car, put on a black leather coat and drove away.

Rains delay big umbrella show

HITACHI-OTA, Japan — Conceptual artist Christo decided Monday to postpone his mammoth umbrella displays in Japan and California after heavy downpours in Japan threatened to wreck six years of painstaking preparation.

I know it sounds crazy, but what if we opened one of the big umbrellas.

Ada Kring, 67-year-old Orick resident, dies at age 94

Hmmm, she was 67 years old, yet she died at age 94.
There's 27 years missing.
Does director Oliver Stone know about this?

We purchased our Crestwood brand electric blanket right after World War II. Now, it seems every winter we need to twist the thermostat more to warm it up. Does anyone know if that company's in business and, if so, where I might write to it?

—Mrs. Harold ▓▓▓▓,

Only 45 years old? Hey, that should still be covered under warranty, huh?

Correction

In last week's Times-Virginian, in the article on Bill Stone the copy read, "He is a member of Evergreen Baptist Church."

This was an error. It should have read, "He is a member of Evergreen Baptist Church."

We regret the error.

I'm glad we cleared that up.

② THAT'S ENTERTAINMENT!

People who live in major metropolitan areas such as New York and L.A. often assume there's no cultural activity to be had in "small-town America." But as these next headlines show, they couldn't be more wrong.

Turkey Testicle Fest

Sample some deep-fried, beer-batter-dipped turkey testicles from 1:30 to 6:30 p.m. Saturday during the 13th annual Turkey Testicle Festival at Union Street Station bar at Illinois 2 and 72 in Byron.

Hmmm, I'm getting hungry already.

Workshop is scheduled on manure management

See, it's *not* just shoveling. There's management involved.

Waste Team Dominates Chili Fest

For the third year in a row, the Churchville Toxic Waste Team has won the Waynesboro chili contest.

Hey, this tastes funny...

Hazardous Waste
breakfast June 6

Hmmm, this dioxin is good.
Could I have a bit more of that medical waste?

Film 'Pants of Glory' offered as tonight's co-op library fare

ONE OF THE GREATEST films ever made, Stanley Kubrick's "Pants of Glory," is the second of the Alabama Film Co-Op's series of classic war films this winter.

Hey, didn't Gary Hart star in that?

17 **Historia USA**
29 **Eye on South Florida (R)**
33 **WGN Monsters**   A cou-
ple fears its fanged, clawed infant son is the neighborhood
slasher.
34 **To Be Announced**

I'm sure their fears are groundless.

"Most sensitive headline" department:

Class For Fatsos

MARSHALL University's Office of Student Health Education Programs will sponsor a weight-loss class on Mondays from 3 to 4:30 p.m., beginning January 29 in Memorial Student Center.

SPCA holds
flea sale

I'm glad they're giving them away,
rather than having them put to sleep.

Run and Bike Ride: Tulsa Wheelmen's "For Fitness Run and Ride," run at 11:30 a.m., cycling 20-30 miles at 13-17 miles-per-hour at noon, 58th Street parking lot, River Parks. <u>Anyone welcome to skip the running or the cycling.</u>

Is it okay if we just stay home and eat donuts?

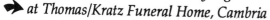
CPR in a funeral home? Is it *really* in their best interests to show you how to do this properly?

▶ **SUNDAY in the East Bay:** A free, guided bird identification walk led by Elsie ████████ will visit several regional parks. Meet at 8:30 a.m. at the parking lot at <u>Kentucky Fried Chicken</u>

BIRDS! GO BACK! IT'S A TRICK! LOOK OUT!

FREE EYE SCREENING
&
BLOOD PRESSURE CHECKS
FOR SENIORS

Date: Monday July 18

Time: 9:00 am – 1:00 pm

Place: ST. Patricks
105 Superior

FREE COFFEE & DONUTS! ←

Ah, coffee and donuts.
Mother Nature's original health food.

Moses to speak
at senior center

Moses? This must be a *really* senior center.

③ NOW WHY DIDN'T I THINK OF THAT?

From our nation's newspapers, we learn the latest scientific discoveries, the results of important surveys, and the opinions of our most learned citizens. Take these headlines, for example:

VOLCANO: NO BARE FEET ALLOWED

Psychopaths unpredictable

♫ They're kooky and they're spooky. They're altogether ooky... ♫

Don't use poison ivy to decorate

Now you tell me.

Water Houseplants When Soil Is Dry

The Associated Press

How often should you water your plants? As often as they need it.

Is this a slow news day or what?

Putting Mattress on Floor Prevents Fall From Bed

And it looks attractive too.

Suicide may hasten death

But only if done properly.

Sadness Is No. 1 Reason Men and Women Cry

Really? I thought it was tax audits.

G.I. Joe is a doll, court decides

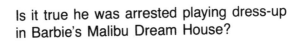

Is it true he was arrested playing dress-up in Barbie's Malibu Dream House?

Appetites Poor Before Execution

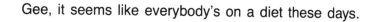

Gee, it seems like everybody's on a diet these days.

Pregnancy problems at Memorial school not caused by air

BRUNSWICK — Environmental conditions at Memorial Elementary School did not cause pregnancy complications for teachers there, a physician reported this week.

Hmmm, it's not the air... You don't think the *boys* are involved, do you?

Farm forecasters predicting a good year, or possibly a bad year

Experts. Sometimes you have to use them.

④ LAW AND ORDER

Mahatma Gandhi once said, "All crime is a kind of disease and should be treated as such." Such is the perversity represented by the following headlines that we can only shudder in response, and hope that a cure is at hand.

Police called in to quell librarians

Toronto Sun
Tempers flared at the U of T yesterday when striking library technicians tried to prevent people from entering the John Robarts Library.

Johnson, call the Captain! More mace!

Man hospitalized; police say wife sat on his head

The Journal staff

A 40-year-old North Side man who police said was pinned by his wife of 300 pounds when she sat on him during a domestic dispute was listed in critical but stable condition Saturday at St. Michael Hospital.

That's what you get for reading *The Joy of Sex*.

...TALLAHASSEE — Psychiatric evaluation has been ordered for Marshall Ledbetter Jr., 22. He's charged with barricading himself in Capitol office Friday and demanding 666 jelly doughnuts and 20-inch vegetable pizza with extra jalapenos before surrendering.

666 jelly doughnuts? Gee, do you think he missed that free blood pressure test? (See page 47)

Clown offered microwave to man for killing his wife

VAN WERT, O. (AP) — A professional clown told a hit man that he would give him a microwave oven if he would kill his wife, a Van Wert County sheriff's investigator said yesterday.

Normally, it would have taken an hour to kill her.
But with the microwave, he could do it in ten seconds.

Two charged in theft of laxatives

MARKHAM — A man and woman from Chicago were charged Tuesday with attempting to steal nearly $1,000 in laxatives from a Homewood drugstore.

$1,000 in laxatives? Wouldn't it have been simpler to switch to a high-fiber diet?

Robbers run away with victims' pants

TORONTO — Armed robbers stole $100,000 in cash and jewelry and about 20 pairs of pants during a robbery at a North York social club on the weekend.

Two men, one wielding a shotgun and the other a handgun, burst into the Abbruzzi Club late Saturday afternoon.

They fired several shots into the ceiling, then ordered the 20 male patrons — no women were present — to take off their pants. The robbers grabbed cash and jewelry and fled in a car belonging to one of the victims. The car was later recovered.

"The men were totally humiliated," a Metro police spokesman from 31 Division said — especially because the first officers at the scene were women. "They showed up to find a bunch of (men) standing outside in their skivvies."

So *that's* what happened to Ted Kennedy.

Man charged with using police desk as bathroom

A 41-year-old Portland man was arrested early Monday morning after he entered the Portland Police Department lobby and urinated on the front desk.

Hey, you don't think this guy was involved in that laxative theft, do you?

Deer breaks into shoe store, escapes down Moose Street

I guess he figured nobody would look for a deer on Moose Street.

Postal worker who killed 4 said to have 'disliked people'

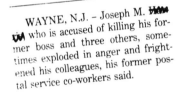

WAYNE, N.J. – Joseph M. ~~Hann~~ ~~M~~ who is accused of killing his former boss and three others, sometimes exploded in anger and frightened his colleagues, his former postal service co-workers said.

Police officials say he would have killed more, but working for the Post Office as he was, he was a little slow.

'Moody' woman arrested in dismemberment of boyfriend

Have I got a roommate for her. (See page 9)

Blind man robs bank, can't find way out

VALLEJO, Calif. — A blind man who handed a threatening note to a bank teller and collected $105 was arrested after he asked her to help him leave the building, police said

Step one: plan ahead.

Breast Implants Seized by Marshals

That could be painful, couldn't it?

Police find TV, lock it in jail

Police locked up a television set early today.

Patrolmen Michael Driscoll and Sean Burke said they were sent to Sullivan and Maginnis avenues for a report of two men trying to steal a television.

When they arrived they found a Sanyo color television sitting on the corner, but no one around.

After checking the area for evidence of a housebreak, the patrolmen took the television back to the police station and locked it in a jail cell.

This cell should straighten you out. And *no* TV privileges!

Police car
hits cow in
line of duty

I guess when the cow refused to pull over,
the officer had no choice.

Cops Gets Burglar to Drop His Pants, Then Pinch Him

Whakatane, New Zealand

The security camera did not clearly register the service station burglar's face. But it did capture the distinctive stripes of his underwear when he bent over to pick up dropped groceries.

Police Sergeant Tony Moller said yesterday that after several eyewitnesses identified the man, police went to question him.

The man at first denied having anything to do with the looting of the station and its food mart. Then they asked him to drop his trousers.

Moller said the evidence was evident, and the man admitted to the crime.

Man in bra, black lace stirs police suspicion

You know, Muldoon, I can't put my finger on it, there's just something about that guy...

Would-be cop arrives for police test in stolen car

THE ASSOCIATED PRESS

Chicago

Arthur Gloria wanted to be a policeman so much he drove a stolen car to take the police exam.

Police said Gloria, 20, had no way to get to the South Side test site Saturday, so he accepted a friend's offer to lend him a stolen car.

Gee, I wonder if he used crib notes?

Suspect in bank robbery was either man or woman

Man gets probation for violating probation

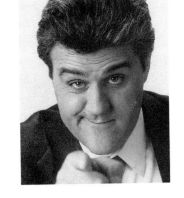

And if you're caught again, more probation!

Cop on tractor nabs 43 speeders

Associated Press

COLLINSVILLE, Ill. — State troopers are taking to deep cover as highway maintenance workers on tractors and hitchhikers with suitcases to nab speeders.

Sergeant Dave Jung said he caught 43 speeders Monday in two hours sitting on a tractor with a radar gun and a two-way radio.

He has also posed as a hitchhiker along the highway with the radar in a suitcase, he said.

Oh, sure, you unhook that tiller and those things really move.

Man fires shots from apartment

Police were trying to convince a rifle-bearing man holed up in his second-floor city apartment to surrender his weapon early this morning.

The man, identified only as "Jerry" by police and neighbors, had fired two shots from his apartment at ▓▓▓▓▓▓▓▓▓▓. One shot was fired inside the apartment about 11:30 p.m.; another shot was fired out the window about 12:30 a.m.

No one was hit by the gunfire. One officer said he heard the second shot pass over his head.

A man called York County Control between 10:30 and 11 p.m. to report that his roommate was about to commit suicide.

City police reported to the scene around 11:30 p.m. and restricted traffic on Commerce, Simpson and Albemarle streets. The city's Quick Response Team followed about 1 a.m.

The "Quick Response" Team took 2½ hours? Maybe they need more tractors.

Cablevision of 922 Waltham Street reported a yellow trailer was stolen sometime between April 17 and two years ago.

Hurry, call the Quick Response Team.

Nashua Man Faces Life Sentence for Murder

Juan D. ~~Rodriguez~~ is in the New Hampshire State Prison, facing a maximum life sentence after his conviction Tuesday of second-degree murder in the 1989 Nashua stabbing death of Jose C. Aldaba of Manchester.

~~Rodriguez~~, 25, of 55 Worcester St., Nashua, was found guilty by a Hillsborough County Superior Court jury of five women and seven men after a three-week trial.

~~Rodriguez~~ took the stand in his own defense, testifying he couldn't have killed Aldaba because at that time he was stabbing another man from Lowell. He conceded, under cross-examination by the state, that he never reported that stabbing to police.

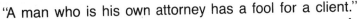

"A man who is his own attorney has a fool for a client."
—*Anonymous*

For some, it's the main reason to buy a newspaper. Where else can you find six copies of *Playboy* and a garden hose listed as an "Estate Sale"? Where else can you find a deal on secondhand wallpaper, or a lead on that lost lint brush? It's because the range of ads in this next chapter is so wide that we refer to it as:

A DIFFERENT CLASS OF CLASSIFIEDS

Rabbit: back legs can't move, but good pet.

Buy two. Make bookends.

I WANT YOU TO TAKE MY MOTHER INTO YOUR HOME & Take Care Of Her.

And when you're through with that,
I've got some more chores for you.

For Sale: 55 gallon aquarium. Does not hold water. Need one that does.

Hmmm, an aquarium that doesn't hold water. Will you throw in the dead fish?

Attention Teenagers

Tired of being hassled
by your stupid parents?
Act now! Move Out ! Get a Job!
Pay your own bills while you still
know everything!!!

Why do I think my dad had something to do with this?

And for Pete's sake, make sure it's before Wednesday.

LOST & FOUND

LOST IN PIOCHE on April 9, reward offered for return, great sentimental value to me, may be near the bank or post office.
Please call _____

Okay, I'll return it. What did you lose?
Hello . . . Hello?

LOST: Pit Bull, friendly, answers to "Gator," wearing a black spiked collar, Harrison City/Manor Rd. area.

ALSO LOST: Owner, affectionate, answers to name "Charlie Manson."

FOUND-female Doberman, 1½ years, florescent color, 2nd/Lewis.

Last seen in Chernobyl area.

FOR SALE: One male, once female, part Chow Chow, seven weeks old. Call ████-████.

Quick, buy it now before it changes again.

Electrolux Vacuum Model G Reconditioned. Runs like new. $50.00. Won't last ← long. Call Dave

Gee, I wonder what kind of guarantee you get with that?

1957 FORD PICK-UP

All original except for motor and auto. trans. Body in good shape, has primer. Have all engine parts except fan and radiator. Needs back window, seat, drive shaft & lots of work!! $400 firm. ███████ after 6:20 pm. & on Weekends.

Actually, the horn doesn't work either.

> Beautiful wedding dress, never used, fits 7-9, $200/OBO; wanted: maternity clothes, 840-3384, Betty.

Trade a wedding dress for maternity clothes?
Gee, I wonder what happened?

BELLA'S PIZZA GUARANTEES same day delivery, Roanoke Island.

Same *day* delivery. See, that's what happens when pizza drivers observe the speed limit.

Does this ever happen to you? You open your morning paper and see a headline so tasteless, so vulgar, so off-color that you think:

THEY COULDN'T POSSIBLY MEAN THAT, COULD THEY?

St. Joe needs new 'image' after losing Dick

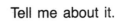
Tell me about it.

Wife tears off testicle in row

LONDON — A woman ripped off one of her husband's testicles with her fingernails during a blazing row, a court was told on Monday.

London transport clerk Lascelles ████████, 45, passed out after seeing the testicle in his wife's blood-covered hand, prosecutor Lisa Matthews told Inner London Crown Court.

He and his wife, were now divorcing, she added.

Hey, that's no reason to split up, huh kids?

Outdoorsman caught in trap while urinating

A man who fell while urinating in the woods was found by Limestone rescue squad workers with a steel trap clamped on his thumb and genitals Thursday night.

Mark A. Tipton, 24, of 7703 W. Redwing Drive told county police he was on Leisure Oaks Park property shooting clay pigeons with a friend. Tipton reportedly lost his footing while urinating and found himself in a painful predicament.

His friend fled after the mishap, Tipton said.

Ow...ow...ow...ow...

Ray Russell-Bell of Schmid Labs of London inflates one of his company's condoms with 12½ gallons of air to demonstrate its strength. The exhibit was part of the Sixth International AIDS Conference in San Francisco.

Talk about
"one size fits all."

Japan's leading condom maker stretching across Pacific

And you thought the condom on the previous page was big.

Three cases of condoms stolen from warehouse for 'recreation'

The Associated Press

ANDERSON, S.C. -- Investigators are looking into the theft of three cases of condoms that an official said apparently were stolen for "recreational purposes."

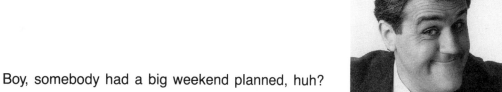

Boy, somebody had a big weekend planned, huh?

Condoms only work if used, study finds

Oh, sure, but who wants a used condom?

How much are alterations?

October is proclaimed Breast Awareness Month

Hey, who came up with this idea—Hugh Hefner?

Sometimes the old ways are the best.

Sexually aggressive teen-age girls

Best gifts for men

Finally, a gift Dad can really use.

Intercourse
News

**A NEWSPAPER OF
INTEREST TO VISITORS
OF THE PENNSYLVNIA
DUTCH COUNTRY**

Hmmm, *Intercourse News*.
I guess this tells what's *really* going on with those Amish people.

Virgin shortage beleaguers CAAC stewardess hunt

Hong Kong, June 28 (Reuter) Mainland China's national airline faces a shortage of stewardesses due to a lack of healthy virgins, the Hong Kong-based Ming Pao Daily News said on Friday.

While there are plenty of applicants many are unhealthy, nearsighted, or no longer virgins, Civil Aviation Administration of China (CAAC) officials were quoted by the Chinese-language newspaper as saying.

Virgin shortage? We've got to stop Geraldo, Wilt Chamberlain, and Ted Kennedy *now*.

Sex may keep legislature in session

Tired of Paris?
Sick of Rome?
Bored with London?

Outhouse tour offers local lore

ANNVILLE — Curiosity seekers yesterday had a front-row seat to outhouse history.

"I didn't know there was so much interest in our subject," said Tanya ████████ a member of Friends of Old Annville, which organized the commode confab called "Lebanon County's First Outhouse Talk and Walk."

Group members decided to sponsor the tour after joking about it for years. They even brought in Gus ████████ of Dillsburg, who shot pictures of myriad latrines for a recent book on outhouse history.

████████ a former employee of the Pennsylvania Historical and Museum Commission and a font of bathroom humor, said the outhouse, in its prime, rarely lent itself to levity.

"They were a very practical necessity that were taken very seriously," he told a rapt crowd that laughed nervously at every off-color quip and body-function euphemism.

"In our grandparents' day, there was no outhouse humor. And if there was, it wouldn't come in the house," he said during a privy-filled slide presentation before the tour.

The extravaganza, co-sponsored by a plumbing company, also featured a "Design-A-Privy" contest

See OUTHOUSES — Page B3

Patriot-News/Ted Anthony

AMERICANA — 94-year-old Herman ████████ preserved his privy.

"That's the last time I go to Taco Bell" department:

Emergency rooms evacuated as man gives off lethal gas

Perth, Australia, July 10 (AP) The emergency rooms of two hospitals were closed after lethal gas leaked from a man who had swallowed pesticide tablets.

The toxic fumes caused Swan Districts Hospital staff in suburban Perth to be evacuated and about 15 patients to be moved from the emergency room of Royal Perth Hospital.

The Tuesday incident also prompted a big fire brigade operation at Royal Perth, with police called in to close off roads in the vicinity. The gas is inflammable as well as toxic.

Several doctors, nurses and ambulance officers were treated for fume inhalation.

Gas odor traced to passenger after emergency landing

FORT MYERS, Fla. (AP) — The pilot of a Braniff Airways flight made an emergency landing and all 47 passengers slid down chutes after people smelled gasoline on board — but the odor was later traced to a man's pants leg.

He was on his way to see his brother at the hospital.
(See previous page.)

Listen, honey.
First we'll pick up some
pork and beans,
then maybe a few burritos,
and I know a nice place
we can stay...

Under a new Casa Grande city ordinance, residents are no longer permitted to throw used underwear in the trash. It must be taken to the office of the city manager for proper disposal.

Disposing of used underwear?
Boy, you thought you hated your job...

HAVE GUN, WILL TRAVEL

In their wisdom, the framers of the Constitution asserted the right of all Americans to "keep and bear arms." Unfortunately, some Americans aren't as bright as others—as the following headlines show.

Sleepy woman shoots herself in face in case of 'mistaken identity'

KEY WEST, Fla. (AP) — A Navy worker who shot herself in the face while in bed blamed the accident on sleepy confusion between two objects she keeps under her pillow — her asthma medication dispenser and a .38-caliber revolver.

"I didn't even know I had hold of the gun until it went off," Vicki ██████, 38, said Tuesday night from her hospital bed.

It's a good thing she wasn't reaching for the Preparation-H.

Police say mother shot son after he threw holiday ham

NORTH LITTLE ROCK, Ark. (AP) — A woman shot her son after he threw her Thanksgiving ham to the floor, stomped on it and threw the pan at her, police said.

So I guess we can forget about the candied yams?

Man charged in shooting over haircut

ORANGE PARK — Police have charged an Orange Park man with attempted murder in a shooting investigators said was triggered by a dispute over a haircut.

Willie ███████, 49, of the 800 block of Floyd Circle is charged with shooting 41-year-old Wilbert Carter in the hand about 7 a.m. Wednesday at the railroad tracks near Floyd Circle and Brown Avenue, said Orange Park Lt. James Boivin.

Carter, of the 800 block of Kingsley Ave., was treated and released at Humana Hospital Orange Park for a bullet wound to his hand. He was shot with a .22-caliber pistol, Boivin said.

Boivin said ███████ is charged with attempted murder, possession of a firearm by a convicted felon and possession of a firearm in the commission of a felony. He was in the Clay County Jail on $50,003 bond yesterday.

Boivin said Carter gave ███████ a haircut four days ago. ███████ told Carter that the haircut was so bad he had to shave his head.

███████ told officers that he shot Carter when he kept "picking on him" about the haircut despite warnings to stop, Boivin said.

No one should ever shoot anyone over a bad haircut.
Okay, maybe if you're Pete Rose.

Man shoots himself in sleep without awaking self, wife

Oregon City, Oregon, July 7 (AP) A sheriff's deputy shot himself in the leg while having a nightmare that someone was attacking him, authorities said.

Todd ███████, 24, told investigators he apparently grabbed his 9mm semiautomatic pistol from his bedside while having a bad dream Friday morning. He awakened to find he had shot himself.

Neither of them woke up? Bet these two have quite a sex life.

Gun-safety officer shoots self

The Associated Press

OKEECHOBEE — A police officer shot himself in the hand while teaching hand-gun safety to his class, authorities said.

Okeechobee Sgt. Kelley ████, a certified firearms instructor who tests his fellow officers in weapons qualifications, was training a group of women on Sunday when the accident occurred.

He stopped to examine a student's .22-caliber pistol when it fired a bullet through his palm.

Good thing he wasn't teaching safe sex.

Store clerk better after being shot

I think if we knifed him, he might feel even better still.

"How do you handle a hungry man?" department:

Man forced to cook spaghetti at gunpoint

A Los Gatos man was arrested early Thursday morning after he reportedly went on a rampage which included forcing his roommate to make spaghetti at gunpoint.

FOR BARGAIN HUNTERS ONLY

They're the Holy Grail of every coupon-saver—those once-in-a-lifetime bargains that could have been missed if it weren't for a careful reading of the 79 advertising circulars the average American receives each week. Think you've spotted every discount to be had? Well, take a look at these...

Mr. Cinnamon

Buy a Single
Get a FREE Baby
Expires Nov. 15, 1991

OR

$1.00 OFF
½ Dozen Babies
Expires Nov. 15, 1991

Mr. Cinnamon

Not good with any other coupon or offer.

I have no idea who Mr. Cinnamon is, but I suggest Social Services contact him immediately.

That's $250 with kids. And if you don't have kids,
see Mr. Cinnamon on the previous page. He'll give you a dollar off.

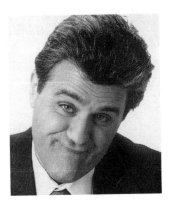

I think Mr. Goodwrench should stick to cars.

Hello, Mr. Johnson, I'm bankrupt,
have bad credit, and am in repossession.
Mr. Johnson, are you there? ...
Mr. Johnson? ... Mr. Johnson?

NEED A CAR?

Nobody Walks Away

NO CREDIT?
BAD CREDIT?
BANKRUPTCY?
REPOSSESSION?
NO CASH DOWN
REQUIRED*

Bank Financing Available
EVERYONE CONSIDERED
EVERYONE DRIVES
➤ *MUST QUALIFY
Call
MR. JOHNSON

Members Of
AA AUTOMOTIVE
ENTERPRISES

> One Million dollar bill
> Authentic, $18.95.
> Call 534-6295.

Uh... I'll give you $17.95.

Ah, I think I'll go across the street. Their free dinner is only $8.

NEW LISTING. Greater North Bay quad-level has seen extensive remodeling. Over $15,000 in exterior and interior improvements. 4 BRs, fireplace, new deck, 2 car attached garage. Asking **$119,000.** James Dickert, **HERITAGE REALTY,** 633-3548/886-4400 **11-144**

Buy now before it tips over.

Call Charles Keating
for details.

SOUTHWEST SAVINGS'
1 YEAR CERTIFICATE
OF DEPOSIT

0.00%

	Annual Rate	Annualized Yield
$500 minimum deposit	0.00%	0.00%

SAFE·SECURE·INSURED

For up-to-the-minute rate information on any Southwest certificate of deposit.
call our 24-hour Rateline toll-free: ▮▮▮▮▮▮▮▮ (▮▮▮▮▮▮▮▮▮▮).

SOUTHWEST SAVINGS

**Accounts insured
to $100,000**

Interest compounded quarterly. Rate subject to change. **Substantial interest penalty for early withdrawal.**
Annualized yield assumes principal and interest remain on deposit and rate remains constant for one full year.

SENIOR CITIZENS
(AGE 50 AND OLDER)
DISCOUNTS

● **Savings are now available at Lake Lawn Park Mausoleum and Metairie Cemetery** with monthly payments as low as $17.72.

● **Save** by doing now what has to be done — sooner or later.

● **Convenience** with additional savings. Lake Lawn Metairie Funeral Home is the only funeral home in the New Orleans area that is located within its own cemetery.

● **Act Now** — Offer limited.

* 12% APR, amount financed $1090, $17.72 for 96 months with a $100.00 down payment. Final Payment $17.32. Total

THE SIMPLICITY PLAN™

● The Simplicity Plan™ offers simple programs to make all phases of funeral arrangements before death.

● With the Simplicity Plan™ you have peace of mind knowing your wishes have been permanently written.

● **There is even a Simplicity Plan™ that will cost you nothing until after death.**

amount financed with interest $1700.72. Discounts apply only to selections made before need.

Nothing until after death? Do you really want these people hounding you in the afterlife?

Hey guys, a free shotgun with purchase of sewing machine.
Perfect for the transvestite hunter!

137

44^{99}

TIRE SWING
No. 06-504-054

Tire not included.

Tree sold separately.

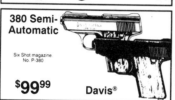
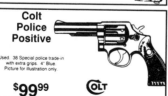

(139)

HICKORY HOUSE

Take Mom out to eat for Her Special Day

Gift Certificates also available

→ CLOSED SUNDAYS and MOTHER'S DAY

▬▬▬▬▬▬, W'loo ▬▬▬▬▬

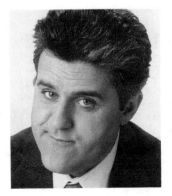

What special day we talking about? Flag Day?

◆ THE VASECTOMY CLINIC ◆

**Celebrates Fathers
on this Special Day**

Charles L. Wilson, M.D.
Certified ◆ American ◆ Board ◆ of ◆ Family ◆ Practice

Shouldn't you call these people if you *don't* want to celebrate Father's Day?

People who are blind can rent cars from Hertz

People who are blind or visually impaired and rent a car from Hertz can do so now easier than ever.

Uh, I guess you'll be wanting the collision coverage, sir.

Oh, geez!
Honey, we're going
to have
to turn around.
We forgot to prearrange
our funeral.

Before you leave for the winter...

Did you remember to:
☐ forward your mail
☐ stop your paper
☐ secure your home
☐ prearrange your funeral

Many people don't think to contact their local funeral home before traveling.
If a death occurs away from home, would you know what to do?

Pre-planning allows:
☐ Protection from funeral cost inflation ☐ Less stress for those you love
☐ Complete transferability anywhere ☐ Comfort of working with a local professional

With no cost
or obligation,
call your
nearby neighbors
for the
answers
you need.

Furry Fall Friends

Easy to make using a straw bale, paper pumpkins, ribbon, oak leaves and mouse parts.

Billy, be careful how you rip those heads off.

HOT DOGS!

39¢

limit 1000
per family.

Only 1,000 per family. I knew there was a catch.

At the request of our customers, Studebaker's will now be:

Open 7 days a week
(Including Monday & Tuesdays)

➤ *Studebaker's*
RESTAURANT & LOUNGE

But what about Thursday and Friday?

LARGE
SELECTION

ROLL TOP DESKS

HOLDS LEGAL
AND ILLEGAL
SIZE PAPERS

36" - 66"

FROM

$553

5 STAINS
TO CHOOSE
FROM

HURRY FOR BEST SELECTION

Perfect for the gangster in the family.

SMELL LIKE GEORGE WASHINGTON.

Caswell-Massey's Number 6 cologne was George Washington's favorite choice. And over 200 years later, Clevelanders can choose from literally hundreds of wonderful scents and personal care products at

Caswell-Massey, Bath and A-Half, Victoria's Secret, and Dino Palmieri Salon. These and nearly 60 other world class shops and restaurants are waiting to help make you look — and feel — like royalty.

Holiday hours 10-9 daily and 11-6 Sundays.

GALLERIA
AT ERIEVIEW

East Ninth and St. Clair in downtown Cleveland.

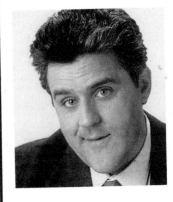

Wooden teeth
sold separately.

Mom, I know you're not dead *yet*, but when I saw this, I thought of you immediately.

BREAKFAST 5 TO7
CRICKETS WORMS

Uh, let me have a plate of worms,
but with the crickets on the side.

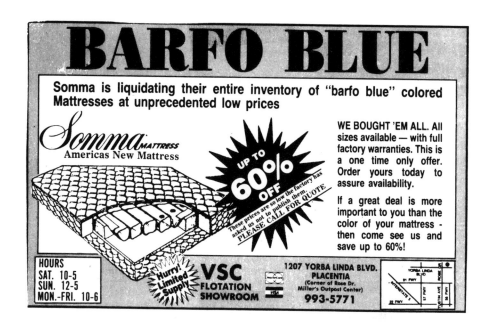

And if you don't like the barfo blue,
it's also available in phlegm and bile.

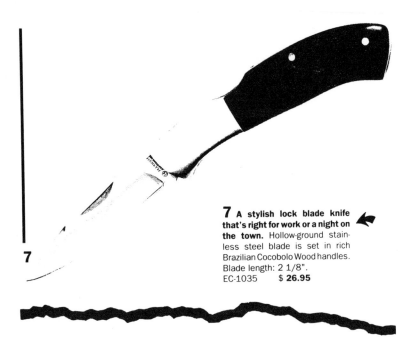

7 A stylish lock blade knife that's right for work or a night on the town. Hollow-ground stainless steel blade is set in rich Brazilian Cocobolo Wood handles. Blade length: 2 1/8".
EC-1035 $ **26.95**

A night on the town?

"Please don't rob me. Please...I'll give you...
Say, that's a beautiful blade you have there."

I'm not sure,
but I'd like to try
the Christie Brinkley
and Cindy Crawford
one more time, please.

IN THIS ISSUE

October 1991   Volume 56, No. 10

IN ORDER TO BETTER SERVE YOU, WE ASK THAT YOU BUS YOUR OWN TABLE. THANK YOU

UCDMC

In order to eat better, I will cook at home. Thank you.

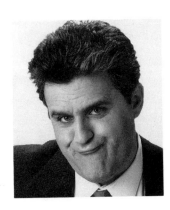

WHAT'S UP, DOC?

A great man once said, "He who has health has hope, and he who has hope has everything." For the current state of health, we have to thank those tireless members of the medical establishment—skillful physicians all—who labor day in and day out to bring us the latest in medical procedures. Take the following, for example:

PATIENT #3 SEVERE BACK PROBLEMS

To save severed foot, it's sewn to his arm

PARIS — Surgeons claimed success yesterday after grafting a severed foot onto a man's forearm.

The unidentified patient fell onto the subway tracks as a train was pulling into the station and the foot was cleanly cut off. Rescue workers found the foot and whisked it to the hospital along with the man.

"There I was, confronted with a foot in perfect condition and a stump that needed several weeks to heal before the foot could be sewn back on," said Dr. Maurice ████████, who headed a team of 10 doctors in the six-hour operation.

If the legs heals properly — it could take from three weeks to three months — ████████ said he will reattach the foot to the stump.

"The patient should be able to walk normally. Without the temporary graft, amputation would have been necessary," he said.

████████ said the patient was under sedation and did not know he had undergone the surgery, which was authorized by the victim's family. The results of the surgery were shown on TV: The swollen, bloodstained foot resting above the hand, which was uninjured.

Oh, sure, you'll walk funny for a while...

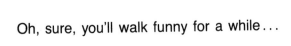

Construction Supervised by:

Groin Extensions

U.S. Army Corps of Engineers

Philadelphia District

Cape May City, N.J.

Contractor:
Agate Construction Co.
Ocean View, N.J.

Uh, hello, Agate Construction? I'm calling for a friend...

Severed ear to heal on man's thigh

Reuters

LONDON — British surgeons have grafted a man's right ear to his thigh after it was bitten off in a fight.

Doctors explained that the ear was too mangled to stitch back onto the patient's head and will "live" on the leg of Patrick ████, 32, where it will have a better chance to survive.

"The ear was cleaned up as well as could be expected, and was then grafted on to Mr. Neary's right thigh, where it will stay for around five months," Dominic ████ of the Queen Victoria Hospital in southern England said Monday.

"His position will then be assessed again and, hopefully, his ear can be moved to its rightful position."

But, Doctor, I've already got a foot stuck to my arm.

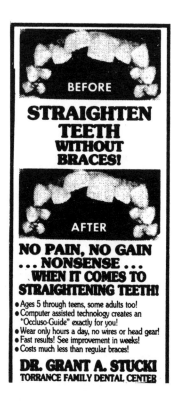

Tell me again, Doctor.
Which is before and which is after?

Isn't this a scene from the movie *Aliens*?

160

No, Doctor, it's not a pinched nerve.
No, it's not back pain. Yes, that's it.

A Complimentary Hernia Exam

Hernias are a common disorder of active people. If you have groin discomfort, pain or bulging — you may have a hernia.

Call the Salt Lake Surgical Center today for a free appointment with one of our Board Certified Physicians. He'll diagnose your problem and offer a treatment program.

If surgery is needed, you'll get quality care at the most competitive price in Utah. And, you'll be back to your normal activities. Quickly.

SALT LAKE SURGICAL CENTER

617 East 3900 South Salt Lake City ▬▬▬▬

Hello, Salt Lake Surgical Center? I'm calling to thank your Dr. Johnson for the complimentary hernia exam. What do you mean, you don't have a Dr. Johnson on staff?

A lot of politicians will tell you that there are *plenty* of jobs out there. Good, high-paying rewarding opportunities. "Stop dillydallying," they'll say, and:

APPLY NOW!

HUBBARD FOODS, INC.

Division of HUBBARD MILLING COMPANY
ALTURA, MINNESOTA 55910

<u>We have an opening for a turkey inseminator.</u>
Job consists of planting semen, chasing and
catching of turkeys.
Experience preferred, but will train.
Position is full time and may include benefits
after trial period.
The wage will be between $5.00 and $8.00 an
hour, depending on experience.
Send resume to address above.
Any questions may be directed to the Personnel Office
507-796-6801.
E.E.O.

Well, I don't know. Do you have to wear a jacket and tie?

★

'THE
OPPOSITE
SEX'

★

AN
OUTRAGEOUS,
PROVOCATIVE,
ENTERTAINING
TV GAME SHOW
PREMIERING
IN JUNE,
SEEKS
PERSONABLE,
OUTGOING,
OPINIONATED
MEN & WOMEN
WHO ARE SEEKING
FUN & MONEY.

KNOWLEDGE
NOT ESSENTIAL

BARRY & ENRIGHT PROD.

★

Baffled by "The Love Connection"?
Find "Studs" too demeaning?
This may be the show for you.

> **TEACHER**
> Full time, Calvary Christian School,
> for potty training 2 year old class.
> Degree preferred, experience
> necessary. Mon.-Fri. 9-5, 381-0256

Well, first of all, I've gone to the bathroom on my own for a few years now...

WING WALKER WANTED

NO EXPERIENCE NECESSARY
EQUAL OPPORTUNITY EMPLOYER
ON THE JOB TRAINING PROVIDED

The Flying Circus

TRYOUTS
Saturday, July 21, 10:30am

THE FLYING CIRCUS
Off Rt. 17 between Warrenton and Fredericksburg, Va.
Call: John King,

Must
Be Over
21

It's those tryouts that are the killer.

Learn new skills, travel, meet other people with gas...

HELP WANTED

MATURE INFANT TO WATCH INFANT live-in my home room and board plus salary, non-smoker, some light housekeeping (415)

How about an immature adult? Is that okay?

35 applicants line up for Lord's old job

Okay, tell me the part about the Flood again...

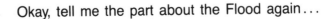

You've met them before. They're the type of people who drink out of bottles marked "Toxic," or drop their hairdryers in the tub while taking a bath, or get their feet caught in wood mulchers. They don't mean to do it. It's just that they've always been:

THEIR OWN
WORST ENEMY

RIDE AT YOUR OWN RISK

DO NOT STAND UP

Woman runs over herself with car

BATAVIA — Finders keepers, losers weepers — or so the saying goes. But all finds do not turn out to be treasures, a Batavia resident recently discovered.

Gloria ████, 52, of 320 Douglas Road, was injured at 12:51 p.m. Thursday — by her own car. Batavia police Lt. Dennis Thomas said ████ was driving north on Randall Road, just north of McKee Street in Batavia, when she spotted a belt in the middle of the road.

She pulled up alongside the belt, keeping her foot on the brake, he said. When ████ reached over to pick up the belt she fell out of the car and the vehicle, which was still in drive, rolled over her leg, he said.

Her grandson quickly put his hand on the brake, stopping the car, Thomas said. A passerby noticed the disabled pair and helped put the car into park, he said.

████ remained under observation Thursday afternoon at Mercy Center Hospital in Aurora, listed in good condition.

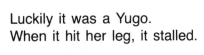

Luckily it was a Yugo.
When it hit her leg, it stalled.

Man shoots self in head, but doesn't know it

No knowledge, eh? Well, I think we've found a contestant for "The Opposite Sex." (See page 165)

Man ticketed for DWI on a lawnmower

KEWANEE, Ill. — A man was charged with drunken driving after riding a lawnmower into the path of a freight train, police said.

Michael ▮▮▮▮▮ had used the 5-horsepower riding mower for transportation after his license was suspended for drunken driving five years ago, said detective Joe Cervantez.

Although he was charged with drunk driving, police did point out that all the weeds between the tracks were neatly cut and trimmed.

What better way to salute the diversity that makes America great than to present the following photos? As much as the headlines they *seem* to illustrate, these pictures capture the nobility of our citizenry and their ingenuity in the face of adversity.

DIRECTOR

Surrogate grandmother gives birth to twins

ABERDEEN, S.D. (AP) — The first American woman to serve as a surrogate mother for her daughter gave birth this morning to her grandchildren — a boy and a girl.

At least it'll be a good-looking family.

"Stalking the wild, bald Caucasian male" department:

GLOBE PHOTO / PAM BERRY

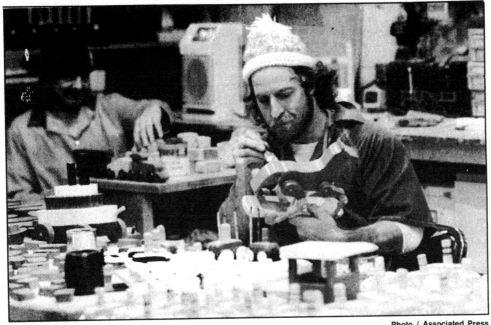

Santa's elves in jail

Bush's Physical Condition 'Incredible,' Doctor Says

You wanna cough again, Mr. President?

"I can't understand why we haven't caught anybody" department:

Once bitten

Agents conduct prostitution sting

Upscale escort services raided

TAMPA, Fla. (AP) — Federal agents raided high-priced call girl escort services around the country, culminating a two-year, $2.5 million money-laundering sting, authorities said Thursday.

AP Laserphoto

Space shuttle launch delayed by equipment

CAPE CANAVERAL, Fla. (AP) — Failed navigation equipment on space shuttle Columbia postponed until at least Wednesday a biomedical research mission involving seven astronauts, 30 rats and a crowded nursery of jellyfish.

I always wondered how astronauts washed their hair in space.

Greyhound faces loss of newly hired replacement drivers as strike continues

Hey, it's still better than taking the bus.

▼

Sexologists meet for multiple orgasm talks

Orgasms in the news: An entertaining dispatch from the frontiers of science, by Steve Coll of The Washington Post:

About 500 self-described sexologists from far corners of the globe, including many from the United States, gathered in a New Delhi hotel this week to attend what organizers called the world's first international conference on the orgasm.

Prakash Kothari, an Indian sex therapist who was the chief sponsor of the meeting, explained its purpose and tenor by saying he was "not just organizing a conference on orgasm. It's also a celebration of orgasm." . . .

The biggest butts of the year: The Center for Media and Public Affairs, which watches what we're watching, has tabulated and indexed 3,025 jokes about public subjects told last year on "The Tonight Show," "Late Night With David Letterman" and "The Arsenio Hall Show."

The 20 people who most often became the butt of jokes in 1990 were: Dan Quayle (162), George Bush (147), Saddam Hussein (137), Marion Barry (83), Ronald Reagan (65), Mikhail Gorbachev (64), Manuel Noriega (56), David Souter (37), Neil Bush (17), Jim and Tammy Bakker (16), Barbara Bush (15), Andy Rooney (14), Joseph Hazelwood (13), Charles Keating (12), Ayatollah Khomeini (12), Imelda Marcos (12) and Michael Dukakis (11).

Suspect arrested in local burglary

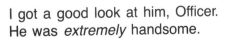

Journal Photo By JEFF KNOX

Comedian and part-time "Tonight Show" host Jay Leno performs for a packed house in Western Hall Saturday night. The performance was the highlight of Parents' Weekend at Western Illinois University. Other events included a Sunday morning brunch in the Union and Saturday

I got a good look at him, Officer. He was *extremely* handsome.

JEFF EARLE/Special to The News Chronicle

Jasmin ████████, 9, of the Las Virgenes Track Club, tries to clear the high jump bar on Saturday.

All right, Jasmin, we're going to lower it again. I want you to try it one more time, okay?

?

Ah, I don't know, Billy. It looks a little thin...